10649507

Santa's Favorite Golf Jokes

by Santa Claus
and His Helpers:

Russ Edwards and Jack Kreismer

Editorial: Ellen Fischbein

Artwork: Jack Kreismer Sr.

Contributors: Angela Demers and Geoff Scowcroft

Cover and Page Design:
Fred and Diane Swartz

RED-LETTER PRESS, INC.
Saddle River, New Jersey

SANTA'S FAVORITE GOLF JOKES

Copyright © 1998 Red-Letter Press, Inc.

ISBN: 0-940462-64-8

All Rights Reserved

Printed in the United States of America

For information address Red-Letter Press, Inc.

P.O. Box 393, Saddle River, N.J. 07458

INTRODUCTION

*Picture the North Pole in your mind...
the actual North Pole- the thing with the
big "N" on top. Few people realize that it
is, in reality, the flag for the first hole at
Santa's North Pole Golf Course,
affectionately known on the pro tour as
"Augusta-Wind."*

*Yes, it's always freezing cold with ice
and blowing snow everywhere but, when
you play Santa's golf course, we can
always promise you one thing- you'll be
on top of the world!*

*As you tee off with this collection of
golf jokes contributed by the North Pole
Golfer's Association, expect to play a full
18 ho-ho-holes!*

Santa Claus

DEDICATION

There were quite a few of
Santa's "subordinate clauses"
who contributed to this
publication, but there's one
in particular who
Santa thinks should be
singularly recognized.
And that's the late
Jack Kreismer Sr.,
whose artwork
in the front of this book,
as Santa says,
"Covered me to a tee."

This one's for you, Pop.

Jack Kreismer Jr.
PUBLISHER

THE GOLFER'S PRAYER

Now I Lay Me Down To Sleep

I Pray The Lord My Life To Keep

Though I Know You'll Eventually Take My Soul

Please Let Me Prepare At The 19th Hole!

JR, the fabulously wealthy Texan, liked to throw his money around and make an ostentatious show of his wealth. The club members tolerated it well enough until one day JR was being followed around the course by a little man lugging not only JR's solid gold golf clubs, but struggling with an elegantly upholstered sofa as well.

"I say old man," said Mr. Worthington Smythe in a bit of a huff, "don't you think it's a little much to expect your caddie to carry both your clubs and a couch?"

JR gave out with a big guffaw and slapped his knee. "Caddie? Why son, that there's my psychiatrist!"

Golf is not a funeral, though both can be very sad affairs.

—Bernard Darwin,
English writer and golfer

If the following foursome is pressing you,

wave them through and then speed up.

—Deane Beman

Waiting to tee off, two golfers struck up a conversation.

"I have four children," said one duffer proudly.

"Oh my, I wish I had four children," said the other.

"Don't you have any children?" asked his new-found friend sympathetically.

"Yeah I do, eight!"

◆ ◆ ◆

Then there was the one about the dentist who couldn't take any more appointments because he had eighteen cavities to fill.

The golf pro began the lesson by saying, "I'd like to see you swing first. Go through the motion without hitting the ball."

The hacker replied, "That's what I'm taking lessons for!"

◆ ◆ ◆

Nigel spotted a hand frantically waving from a bed of quicksand on a golf course in Botswana.

"I say," he remarked to his companion. "Do you think he's signalling for his wedge?"

◆ ◆ ◆

Then there was the duffer who had a beautiful short game. Unfortunately, it was off the tee.

Anyone who likes golf on television would enjoy watching the grass grow on the greens.

—Andy Rooney

If you can't break 85 you have no
business on the golf course. If you can
break 85 you probably have no business.

—"The Old Farmer's Almanac"

Jim was playing golf with his grandfather and they were on a severely doglegged par 4.

The grandfather said, "You know, when I was your age, I'd aim right over those trees and hit the green every time."

Jim, who was in a tight game with the old master and hungry for victory, took the tip and made a perfect drive which slammed right into the top of one of the 50-foot trees.

"Grandpa," Jim said with frustration. "It didn't work."

"Well," replied his grandfather with a wink, "when I was your age, those trees were saplings."

The castaway used his fifteen years on the tiny island to set up a golf course so he could keep himself amused. When rescue finally came to this coral atoll in the mid-Pacific, far from the shipping lanes, the captain said to the marooned sailor, "I must say, this is quite a nice nine-hole course you've managed here."

"Oh, it's not such-a-much," answered the castaway, gazing dreamily out to sea. "But I am quite proud of the water hazard."

After hitting her third consecutive quadruple bogey, the woman said, "I've never played this badly before."

Her caddie said, "You've played before?"

The only problem with the Senior Tour is that when you're through here, they put you in a box.

—J.C. Snead

I really enjoy doing corporate outings because there are no cuts and I'm low pro every day.

—Dave Stockton

Duffer: How would you have played that last shot?

Caddie: Under an assumed name.

◆ ◆ ◆

Harry was playing a short hole when his drive smacked into a bird which fell right into the cup. This marked the first time ever for a partridge in a par three.

◆ ◆ ◆

Q: Why is golf better than fishing?

A: You don't have to produce anything to prove your story.

Sheldon's tee shot resulted in a horrible slice that flew over to the next fairway, conking a bystander in the head and knocking him cold.

By the time Sheldon and his partner, Rich, arrived, the man was lying unconscious on the ground with the ball between his feet.

"What should I do?" Sheldon blurted out in a panic.

"Don't touch him," said Rich. "If we leave him here, he becomes an immovable obstruction and you can drop the ball two club lengths away."

I'm convinced the reason most people play golf is to wear clothes they would not be caught dead in otherwise.

—Roger Simon

You all know Jerry Ford— the most
dangerous driver since Ben Hur.

—Bob Hope

A small private plane was flying over southwest Florida when all of a sudden the engine died, miles away from any airport. The pilot turned to his wife and said, "Don't worry honey, there're dozens of golf courses in this area. I'll just land on the next one I see."

To which his wife replied, "What do you mean 'don't worry'? I've seen you play. You'll never hit the fairway!"

◆ ◆ ◆

Q: Why is golf a lot like taxes?

A: You drive very hard to get to the green only to wind up in a hole.

A golfer goes to a psychiatrist and says, "My wife thinks I'm crazy because I like plaid golf socks."

"That's not so strange," replies the doctor. "As a matter of fact, I kind of like them, too."

"Really?" exclaimed the patient, excited to find a sympathetic ear. "Do you like yours with chocolate fudge or Hollandaise sauce?"

◆ ◆ ◆

A nd then there was the duffer who was determined to live to be 125. Just once, he wanted to shoot his age.

If a lot of people gripped a knife and fork the way they do a golf club, they'd starve to death.

—Sam Snead

Arnold Palmer is the biggest crowd pleaser since the invention of the portable sanitary facility.

—Bob Hope

HO-HO-HO!

"Father," the young man said to the priest, "is it a sin to play golf on Christmas Day?"

"My son," replied the padre, placing his hand on the fellow's shoulder, "the way you play golf, it's a sin any day."

Fred: I went to see the doctor today.

Red: Really? What did he say?

Fred: He said I can't play golf.

Red: He's obviously been out with you before.

The caddie pointed out a ball in the rough that he claimed was Ralph's.

"That can't be my ball," said Ralph. "It looks way too old."

"You forget sir," the caddie responded. "We've been out here for a very long time."

Then there was the hunter who got a hole-in-one but went crazy trying to figure out how to mount it.

I used to play golf with a guy who cheated so badly that he once had a hole in one and wrote down 0 on the score card.

—Bob Brue

This is a very sophisticated club...

All the greens break toward the hot tub.

—Snoopy
(in "An Educated Slice", by Charles M. Schulz)

Two golfers are standing on the 10th tee. Jerry takes about 20 practice swings, changes his grip five or six times, and adjusts his stance just as much.

"Hey, Jerry! Play, for heaven's sake. We don't have all day," says Chris.

"Hold on a minute, I gotta do this right. See the woman standing up there on the clubhouse porch? That's my mother-in-law and I would like to get off the perfect shot," says Jerry.

Chris looks, and about 250 yards away he sees the woman.

"You must be kidding. You couldn't possibly hit her from here."

A duffer sliced his tee shot right into the woods. Rather than take a penalty, he decided to go for it. Unfortunately, his second shot caromed right off the trunk of a big old oak tree, hitting him right between the eyes and killing him instantly.

The next thing he knew, he was standing before St. Peter at the Pearly Gates.

St. Peter, trying to find his name on the list, said, "Oh, here it is. But according to this, you're not scheduled to die for another 25 years. How did you get here?"

"In two."

How do I address the ball? I say,
"Hello there, ball. Are you going to go
in the hole or not?"

—Flip Wilson

GOLFER'S HOROSCOPE

Aquarius (Jan 20-Feb 18) The Golf Club
Born under the sign of the country club, you are industrious, prosperous and like to wear funny pants. Your idea of excitement is pulling the old "dead mouse in the golfbag" trick on the newest member of the club.

Pisces (Feb 19-Mar 20) The Sand Trap
You are a Child of The Sand Trap. You are innately drawn to the rough and to water hazards. This is because in a former life, you were either Lewis or Clark.

Aries (Mar 21-Apr 19) The Golf Tee
Born under the sign of the tee, you came into the world along with the spring- which explains why the smell of newly mowed grass follows you everywhere. It's all those divots!

Taurus (Apr 20-May 20) The Golf Ball
Born under the sign of the golfball, you tend to be round and dimpled all over.

Gemini (May 21-Jun 21) The Golf Swing
Like all Gemini golfers, you have a tendency to stand too close to the ball. Unfortunately, that's also true after you've hit it.

Cancer (Jun 22-Jul 22) The 19th Hole
The summer heat means that you are one of the chosen children of the 19th Hole. Trading golfballs for highballs, you play a round then buy one.

Leo (Jul 23-Aug 22) The Driving Range
Your life is intimately tied up with the game.
Sadly, the best drive you'll ever make is in a
golf cart.

Virgo (Aug 23-Sep 22) The Scorecard
A Scorecardian, you are good with numbers...
a talent you put to good use in cheating.

Libra (Sep 23-Oct 23) The Water Hazard
Under the sign of the Water Hazard you are
forever losing your ball in the drink. You have
such an amazing ability at finding the water
that your golfing companions refer to your
woods as "diving sticks."

Scorpio (Oct 24-Nov 21) The Golf Shoe
You are tremendously gifted at golf. In fact, you
immediately master any hole you attempt...
especially the ones with windmills.

Sagittarius (Nov 22-Dec 21) The Glove
Though your tee off time is late in the year,
you are devoted to your sport. This is a shame
because, basically, you stink!

Capricorn (Dec 22-Jan 19) The Fairway
Though you have much power, you are horribly
inconsistent. In fact, you would do well to hit
your first drive before deciding which course
you'll be playing that day.

I call my sand wedge my half-Nelson,
because I can always strangle the
opposition with it.

—Byron Nelson

F our old golfers took to the links on a Saturday
morning as they had every week for the past
ten years. The competition was as keen as ever.

On the sixth hole, one of the golfers suddenly
collapsed just as he was about to hit a bunker
shot. As he lay on the ground, one of the other
golfers shouted, "I think Nellie just had a stroke."

Said another player, "Well, just make sure he
marks it on his card."

◆ ◆ ◆

T hen there was the golfer who spent so much
time in the sand traps he was known as
Lawrence of Arabia.

G ertrude and Lily had just met each other and were talking when the subject of golf came up.

Gertrude said, "I'm one of those golf widows, I guess. My husband spends more time on the course than at home."

"I'm a golf widow, too," said Lily.

"Oh, does your husband play a lot, too?"

"No. He tried to play a stroke rather than concede it and was killed when he fell out of a tree."

◆ ◆ ◆

H usband: Wow! A hole-in-one!!!

Wife: Sorry, dear, I missed it. Would you do it again?

I don't have any handicap. I am all handicap.

—President Lyndon B. Johnson

My putting is so bad I could putt it off a tabletop and leave it short, halfway down a leg.

—J.C. Snead

A man tees up at the first hole. All of a sudden, a woman wearing a bridal gown comes running toward him. "You bum! You bum!" she screams.

"Aw, c'mon, dear," he says. "I told you only if it rains."

♦ ♦ ♦

"What's the worst thing a player can do in golf?" the wide-eyed novice asked his instructor.

"Bend the elbow," answered the pro.

"That will mess up your swing, huh?"

The pro nodded and added, "Especially if you start doing it in the clubhouse before the game."

Terry and Joe were teeing off early one summer's day when the usual tranquility of the golf course was shattered by the siren of an ambulance racing to the maternity hospital atop a nearby hill.

"Somebody's getting a big surprise today," remarked Joe.

"I'll say," replied Terry as he lined up his putt. "When I left this morning, my wife's contractions were still at least an hour apart."

Take it from Santa: do you know what happens to naughty little boys who swear all the time? They grow up to be golfers.

Golf is the hardest game in the world to play and the easiest to cheat at.

—Dave Hill

I'd do better if the ball were two feet off

the ground and moving.

—Stan Musial,
Baseball Hall of Famer

Q: What do you call people who see doctors regularly?

A: Caddies

◆ ◆ ◆

The First Lady, a long-suffering widow with a deep contempt for the game, was talking to a professional golfer at a White House reception.

"So, what prompted you to take up golf as a career?" she asked.

"I suppose because my father was a professional golfer," the pro answered amiably.

"Well tell me then, what would you have done had your father been a criminal?" inquired the First Lady.

"In that case ma'am," the golfer smiled, "I'd have become a politician."

And then there's the "scratch golfer." He writes down all his good scores and scratches out all his bad ones.

◆ ◆ ◆

Q: Why do most golfers use carts instead of caddies?

A: Because you can count on your cart but it can't count on you.

◆ ◆ ◆

There are two kinds of people: those who play golf and those who don't. The trouble is, they're usually married to each other.

I never pray on the golf course. Actually, the Lord answers my prayers everywhere except on the course.

—Reverend Billy Graham

*My best score ever is 103. But I've only
been playing fifteen years.*

—Alex Karras,
actor and former football player

A golfer was having a day where he could do no right. At one point with his ball about 200 yards from the green, the duffer sized up the situation and asked his caddie, "Do you think I can get there with a five-iron?"

The caddie responded, "Eventually."

◆ ◆ ◆

Q: What are the four worst words you could hear during a game of golf?

A: "It's still your turn!"

◆ ◆ ◆

Did you ever notice that the same nation which invented golf and called it "fun" also invented bagpipes and called it "music"?

" Your ball hit me in the eye! I'll sue you for five million dollars!"

"I said 'fore'."

"Deal!"

◆ ◆ ◆

Barrington: I say, did you hear what happened to Rockingham?

Hyde-White: No, I'm afraid I haven't.

Barrington: He was awakened in the middle of the night by a burglar and beat the miscreant into submission with a five-iron.

Hyde-White: Do tell. How many strokes?

I'd give up golf if I didn't have so many sweaters.

—Bob Hope

For most amateurs, the best wood in the bag is the pencil.

—Chi Chi Rodriguez

Two old friends, Ken and Tom, ran into each other on the course.

"Say, Tom. I notice you have two caddies. Has your game gotten that bad?"

Tom says, "Nah, it was my wife's idea."

"How's that?" asks Ken.

"She doesn't think I spend enough time with the kids."

One duffer said to another, "After seven years of lessons, 3,000 golf balls and sixteen golf vacations, I finally learned to get some fun out of the game."

"How so?"

"I quit."

Y ou can always tell a true golfer. He has a fake alligator on his shirt and a real crock on his scorecard.

◆ ◆ ◆

B ert: How was your golf vacation?

Ernie: Wonderful. The resort we stayed at was in the South Seas and the entire island was covered in seven different golf courses.

Bert: How did you decide which one to play?

Ernie: I'd just whack a ball off the balcony each morning and whatever course it landed on, that was it.

The players themselves can be classified roughly into two groups — the attractions and the entry fees.

—Jimmy Demaret

The 10 Funniest Golf Quotes

According to SANTA

1. "Ninety percent of the putts that fall short don't go in."

   —Yogi Berra

2. "Once when I was golfing in Georgia I hooked the ball into the swamp. I went in after it and found an alligator wearing a shirt with a picture of a little golfer on it."

   —Buddy Hackett

3. "If it wasn't for golf, I'd probably be a caddie today."

   —George Archer

4. "I learn English from American pros... that's why I speak so bad. I call it PGA English."

   —Roberto deVicenzo

5. "If you pick up a golfer and hold it close to your ear, like a conch shell, you will hear an alibi."

—Fred Beck

6. "I know I'm getting better at golf because I'm hitting fewer spectators."

—Gerald R. Ford

7. "I find it to be the hole-in-one."

—Groucho Marx,
on the most difficult shot in golf

8. "The reason the pro tells you to keep your head down is so you can't see him laughing."

—Phyllis Diller

9. "I had a wonderful experience on the golf course today. I had a hole in nothing. Missed the ball and sank the divot."

—Don Adams

10. "When your name is Zoeller, and so many things are done in alphabetical order, you expect to be last."

—Fuzzy Zoeller

Golf is not a game, it's bondage. It was obviously devised by a man torn with guilt, eager to atone for his sins.

—Jim Murray

The President of the United States was on the golf course with an old army buddy and as they were walking off the 18th green his friend said, "Mr. President, I was wondering if you could get my son a job in the White House?"

"Certainly," replied the Chief Executive. "What does your son do?"

His friend shook his head sadly and said, "Nothing."

"Excellent," replied the President. "Then we won't have to train him."

◆ ◆ ◆

The trouble with playing golf with an Englishman is that every time somebody yells "Fore!" he sits down for tea!

G ale: Played golf with my boss the other day.

Howard: How'd it go?

Gale: Well, on the first hole, the boss topped the ball and only sent it about 20 feet, leaving it 375 yards from the hole.

Howard: What'd you do?

Gale: I conceded the putt.

◆ ◆ ◆

" I hate golf. I hate golf. I hate golf."

"Nice shot."

"I love golf. I love golf. I love golf."

I'm hitting the woods just great, but I'm having a terrible time getting out of them.

—Harry Toscano

Never bet with anyone you meet on the first tee who has a deep suntan, a one-iron in his bag and squinty eyes.

—Dave Marr

Duffer: You perhaps won't believe it, but I once did this hole in one.

Caddie: Stroke or day, sir?

◆ ◆ ◆

"Be honest, caddie," Weinstein said as he teed up his ball on the 18th hole. "Do you see any change in my game since we started?"

The caddie stroked his chin thoughtfully for a moment and replied, "Well sir, they're getting longer."

"My drives?" asked Weinstein.

"No, sir... our shadows."

HO·HO·HO!

Two golfers relaxing at the 19th Hole were going over their Christmas plans:

Harry: I got a new set of golf clubs for my wife the other day.

Barry: Nice trade.

Crumstead was called into Mr. Smithers' office.

"Crumstead...I happen to know that yesterday, when you took off from work because you were supposedly sick, you played golf at the Greenwood Country Club."

"That's not true sir," Crumstead protested, "and I have the fish to prove it!"

If you're stupid enough to whiff, you should be smart enough to forget it.

—Arnold Palmer

If you three-putt the first green, they'll never remember it. But if you three-putt the 18th, they'll never forget it.

—Walter Hagen

Joe shook his head and said, "I'm not too sure about that caddie of mine."

"What's the problem?" asked his buddy, Bill.

"Every darn time I get in the bunker and I ask him for a sand wedge he disappears for a half hour."

"Where's he go?" asked Bill.

"I guess back to the club house," replied Joe. "When he shows up again, he always hands me a ham and cheese on rye."

◆ ◆ ◆

Golfer: How can I cut down on my strokes?

Pro: Take up painting.

Did you hear about the divorce lawyer who did a mailing to all the married male members of the exclusive country club?

She sent out 175 Valentines signed "Guess who?"

◆ ◆ ◆

Charley: Ralph plays a fair game of golf.

George: Yes, but only if you keep your eye on him.

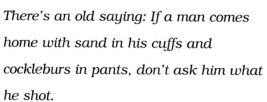

There's an old saying: If a man comes home with sand in his cuffs and cockleburs in pants, don't ask him what he shot.

—Sam Snead

Golfers find it a very trying matter to turn at the waist, more particularly if they have a lot of waist to turn.

—Harry Vardon

You know what happened to the guy who wrote a book called "The Complete List of Golf Terms"?

As soon as it was published, he was arrested for obscenity.

◆ ◆ ◆

Mark threw his golf bag down on the porch and stormed into the house.

"My gosh, what's wrong, honey?" asked his wife, Joann.

"I was dinged 500 bucks by the club for striking my partner."

"For unsportsmanlike conduct?"

"No...for using the wrong iron."

High in the Colorado Rockies near Pike's Peak, Champ and Fred, two avid golfers, came to play the world's most difficult course at Nine Mile Heights. Champ hit a tough lie at the bottom of a crevasse, then caught up with his buddy.

"How many did you take?" asked Fred.

"Two," was the reply.

"Two? I heard four," challenged Fred.

"Two were echoes."

Maybe you've heard about the North Pole golfer who, when on the green, would take a swig from his hip flask to ward off the cold. It became known as the shot putt.

They don't have McDonald's up there.

—John Daly,
on why he doesn't like flying

*It's so ridiculous to see a golfer with a
one-foot putt and everybody is saying
"Shhh" and not moving a muscle. Then
we allow 19-year-old kids to face a game-
deciding free throw with 17,000 people
yelling.*

—Al McGuire

Standing on the tee of a long par three, the confident golfer said to his caddie, "Looks like a four-wood and a putt to me."

The caddie handed him the four-wood with which the golfer topped the ball about 15 yards in front of the tee. Immediately, the caddie handed him his putter and said, "And now for one heck of a putt."

Then there was the cantankerous old golfer who hit a hole-in-one and said, "Great- just when I needed putting practice."

Bismo the Gorilla was making a fortune for his owner. They'd travel around to golf courses and challenge the pro to a round of golf. They always accepted the bet figuring that they could easily beat the muscle-bound primate. That was until Bismo stepped up to the tee and drove the ball 450 yards. Then they'd usually give up, pay the bet and scamper away with their tails between their legs.

One morning, a top-rated country club pro conceded the bet after the gorilla drove the ball 450 yards to the green.

"Just out of curiosity," the pro asked as he forked over the cash, "how does Bismo putt?"

"The same as he drives," said the gorilla's owner. "450 yards."

Golf is essentially an exercise in masochism conducted out of doors.

—Paul O'Neil

Being left-handed is a big advantage. No one knows enough about your swing to mess you up with advice.

—Bob Charles

HO-HO-HO!

Naturally Santa loves all the holiday songs... except one. As an avid golfer, it always gives me the willies to hear the carolers sing, "Over the river and through the woods..."

"Caddie, why do you keep looking at your watch?"

"It's not a watch, sir. It's a compass."

Joe: Did you know that Columbus went around the world in 1492?

Moe: That's not many strokes when you consider the distance.

A minister and his very conservative wife had a great marriage except for his long business trips and lifelong obsession with golf.

One day while he was away, she was cleaning and found a box of mementos in the back of the bedroom closet. In it she found three golf balls and $800.

That night when he called, she asked him the meaning of the three golf balls. He said, "Well, dear I've been keeping that box for twenty years. I'm ashamed to admit it but so great is my passion for the game of golf that occasionally I swear on the course. Every time I use unsavory language, I penalize myself one golf ball."

Shocked that her husband, a man of the cloth, would ever use four-letter words, the wife was at first taken aback but then thought, "Well, three balls means that he's only cursed three times in 20 years. I suppose that isn't so bad."

"All right dear," she said, "I forgive you for your lapses, but tell me, what's the $800 for?"

"Oh that," answered the minister. "I found a guy who buys golf balls at two bucks a dozen."

We're playing a game where the aim is to be below par. It's so wrong for me.

—Stephanie Vanderkellen

At the 19th Hole, two old duffers were nursing a beverage and discussing golf.

"You know what the trouble with this game is?" said Quincy.

"What?" asked Ernie.

"Well, now that I'm far enough in life that I can afford all the new balls I need, I can't hit them far enough to lose them!"

Hacker: Wow! Four-and-a half hours just to play the front nine. You must be tired of carrying that bag.

Caddie: Not really, sir...just of counting.

Doctor: Mr. Feebus, I'm afraid you're suffering from stress. Your nerves are shot.

Golfer: What can I do, Doc?

Doctor: You're going to have to take some time off and relax. Go somewhere that you can get some peace and quiet.

Golfer: Where do you suggest, Doc?

Doctor: I'd recommend the office.

The hardest shot is a mashie at 90 yards from the green, where the ball has to be played against an oak tree, bounces back into a sandtrap, hits a stone, bounces on the green, and then rolls into the cup. The shot is so difficult I have only made it once.

—Zeppo Marx

Some guys get so nervous playing for their own money, the greens don't need fertilizing for a year.

—Dave Hill

Two retired businessmen were out on the links, both complaining of their misfortunes.

"How did you lose your business?" one asked the other.

"It was a fire. It destroyed everything. And you...what happened to your business?"

"Flood," the first responded.

"Flood? Really? How do you arrange a flood?"

You know how you can tell a golfer in church? He's the one who, when he puts together his hands to pray, has the interlocking grip.

Duffernitions

Graphite Shaft: what the guy who cheats on the scorecard gives you

Foursome: the best way to make slowpokes let you play through

Greenskeeper: the guy at the pro shop who keeps all your money

Driving range: if you're playing golf with Gerald Ford, what you want to make sure the hospital is within

Dogleg: what you'll often see just before a water hazard

Handicapped golfer: one who plays with his boss

Practice swing: what you can't claim after yelling, "%&$#@%!"

Scratch golfer: the guy whose bench you'll want to avoid in the locker room

I drew a big gallery today. I was paired with Arnold Palmer.

—Gene Littler

Golf is an open exhibition of overweening ambition, courage deflated by stupidity, skill soured by a whiff of arrogance... These humiliations are the essence of the game.

—Alistair Cooke

On the tenth hole, a foursome was getting ready to tee off when a man came running up to them completely out of breath.

"I say old chaps, I hate to interrupt but I've just gotten word that my wife has fallen seriously ill."

"Bad break old boy," replied one of the men. "Is there anything at all we can do?"

"Well, if you don't mind, you could let me play through."

om runs excitedly into the locker room and holds up a golf ball. "Look at this!" he says.

"Looks like a plain old golf ball to me," says Steve.

"This is no ordinary golf ball," Tom responds. "This is a golf ball that can not be lost."

Steve says, "Yeah, sure. Any ball can be lost."

"Not this one," replies Tom. "It's got a special radar tracking device so that if you hit it in the woods or rough or even the water, you can locate it."

"Oh yeah? Where'd you get this super-duper ball, anyway?"

"I found it."

I play with friends but we don't play friendly games.

—Ben Hogan

The putter is a club designed to hit the ball partway to the hole.

—Rex Lardner

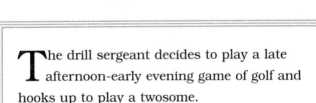

The drill sergeant decides to play a late afternoon-early evening game of golf and hooks up to play a twosome.

Four quadruple bogeys, three triple bogeys and two double bogeys later the sarge's partner says, "When did you take up this game?"

The drill sergeant says, "Nineteen fifty-nine."

"Nineteen fifty-nine?" says the other golfer. "I would think that you'd be able to play a little better than this."

"Whaddya mean?" says the sarge. "It's only twenty-two thirteen right now."

Jenny: Dear, I have bad news and worse news.

Neal: What's the bad news?

Jenny: I ran over your golf clubs.

Neal: What could be worse than that?

Jenny: They were on the front porch at the time.

◆ ◆ ◆

Q: How is golf like fishing?

A: Both mysteriously encourage exaggeration.

Golf is a game in which you claim the
privileges of age, and retain the
playthings of childhood.

—Dr. Samuel Johnson

A Golfer's Christmas Carols*

Yes, there really are such tunes. Limber up your larynx as Santa brings you the words to a couple of them.

O' 19TH HOLE (O' CHRISTMAS TREE)

O, nineteenth hole, O, nineteenth hole

That's where you'll find refreshments sold

O, nineteenth hole, O, nineteenth hole

And where the tallest tales are told

Much better lies than on the links

And bigger after several drinks!

O, nineteenth hole, O, nineteenth hole

That's where you'll find refreshments sold!

O, nineteenth hole, O, nineteenth hole

Where golfers do commiserate

O, nineteenth hole, O, nineteenth hole

But mostly to just fabricate

About those shots you should have seen

And all those rubbings of the green!

O, nineteenth hole, O, nineteenth hole

That's where you'll find refreshments sold...

THE TWELVE DAYS OF CHRISTMAS

On the twelve days of Christmas,
my true love gave to me...

Twelve dozen balls,

Eleven perfect lies,

Ten mulligans,

Nine no brainers,

Eight great excuses,

Seven heaven woods,

Six wooden tees,

Five Golf Vacations!

Four greenies,

Three birdies,

Two spikeless shoes...

And an eagle on a par three!

*A Golfer's Christmas Carols, *officially endorsed by
the North Pole Golfer's Association, is available on
cassette tape from the publishers of this book. Santa,
with a hearty ho ho ho, highly recommends it.*

Some days I felt like Superman and other
days I found I was made of Jell-O.

—Dave Marr

The Sheik of all sheiks was rushed to the hospital for an emergency appendectomy. The attending surgeon expertly removed the organ despite serious complications.

"You saved my life," said the Sheik upon regaining consciousness. "Anything you want is yours."

"That's not necessary," responded the doctor.

"But I insist," said the Sheik.

"Well, okay, I could use a new set of matched clubs."

"Done!" said the Sheik.

A few weeks went by and the busy doctor had forgotten all about the Sheik's promise when a fax arrived. It read: From: The Sheik To: The Good Doctor...I have bought you the new set of golf clubs you requested but am eternally embarrassed and humbled that they sadly do not match. I was appalled to discover that four do not have swimming pools.

Q: What did the ancient Romans yell on the golf course?

A: IV!

♦ ♦ ♦

Joe and Marty were playing in two-ball foursome and Joe drove his tee shot right to the edge of the green on a par three hole. Marty, playing the second shot, chipped it over the green into a bunker. Undaunted, Joe connected and sent it rolling to within three feet of the hole. Marty stepped up and blew the putt, leaving Joe to sink it.

"Do you realize that we took five shots on an easy par three?" an annoyed Joe remarked.

"Yeah," replied Marty, "and let's not forget who took three of them."

Some guys hope to shoot their age. Craig Stadler hopes to shoot his waist.

—Jim Murray

I never exaggerate; I just remember big.

—Chi Chi Rodriguez

"I'd move heaven and earth to break 100 on this course," sighed Phil.

"Try heaven," advised the caddie. "You've already moved most of the earth."

"Man, that Wally cheats," grumbled the golfer.

"Why do you say that?" his buddy asked.

"Today on the fourth hole, he lost his ball in the rough and slyly played a new one."

"How do you know?"

"Because I had his original ball in my pocket."

HO·HO·HO!

At two-foot three, Jingles the elf is the world's smallest golfing fanatic. He plays the North Pole course every chance he gets, out there carrying his tiny little golf bag. You should see him as he takes out his miniature driver, tees up a teensy-weensy ball, takes his itty-bitty swing and hollers, "Two!"

The boss was sitting at the 19th Hole with an old friend, complaining that he couldn't stand playing golf with any of his kiss-up junior executives.

"It drives me mad," said the CEO, taking a sip of his drink. "Every time I yell 'Fore', they chime in with 'He's a jolly good fellow'."

The uglier a man's legs are, the better he plays golf. It's almost a law.

—H.G. Wells

You can, legally, possibly hit and kill a
fellow golfer with a ball, and there will not
be a lot of trouble because the other golfers
will refuse to stop and be witnesses because
they will want to keep playing.

—Dave Barry

A witness in an accident case described himself as "the best amateur golfer in the state of Florida."

"Modest, aren't you," sneered the cross-examining attorney.

"Normally, yes. But now I'm under oath."

Jack Lemmon tells of this one-liner from his caddie:

"I was lying ten and had a 35-foot putt. I whispered over my shoulder, 'How does this one break?' He said, 'Who cares?'"

The widow Applegate called the newspaper to inquire about the cost of a death notice.

"It's six bucks for six words," the classified clerk answered.

The Applegates didn't amass their considerable fortune by throwing that kind of money around so the widow said, "Can't I just get two words—'Applegate dead'?"

"No, I'm sorry, six dollars is the minimum. You still have four words left."

Mrs. Applegate thought for a moment and then added, "Golf clubs for sale."

Golf combines two favorite American pastimes: taking long walks and hitting things with a stick.

—P.J. O'Rourke

Hold up a one-iron and walk. Even God can't hit a one-iron.

—Lee Trevino,
on how to deal with lightning

A panic-stricken golfer charged into the clubhouse, grabbed the pro by the arm and said, "You gotta help me! I was on the ninth hole and I hit a terrible slice. The ball sailed right off the course and bopped a guy riding a motorcycle. He lost control and swerved into the path of a truck. The truck jackknifed, rolled over and broke apart spilling thousands of beehives and now the angry bees are attacking everyone in sight. It's awful! It's a disaster. What should I do?"

The pro answered, "Well, the first thing you need to do is to keep your arms straight and remember to get your right hand a bit more under the club."

Rex had a particularly bad day on the course. Nothing went right and by the time he missed a two-foot putt on the 17th to round his score up to 130, he blew his stack.

He removed his golf clubs from his bag and cracked them over his knees before hurling them into the water.

"I'll never play golf again," he roared.

He then kicked the bag around, tossed that in the water too and, in a super-human burst of rage, he flipped the golf cart over into the lake. At that point, he stomped off toward the clubhouse.

One of the members happened by, just missing the tantrum and innocently asked, "Hey Rex, we need a fourth for tomorrow. Can you make it?"

Rex stopped in his tracks, looked up and said, "What time?"

I'm allergic to grass. Hey, it could be worse. I could be allergic to beer.

—Greg Norman

(A gun is) a recreational tool, like a golf club or a tennis racket. You can kill someone with a golf club, you know.

—Martel Lovelace,
NRA official

A schoolteacher taking her first golfing lesson asked the instructor, "Is the word spelled 'p-u-t' or 'p-u-t-t'?"

"'P-u-t-t' is correct," he replied. "'Put' means to place a thing where you want it. 'Putt' means a usually vain attempt to do the same thing."

Duffer one: What's your handicap?

Duffer two: I'm too honest.

Two old golfers were reminiscing as they played. One pointed towards the woods. "My first girlfriend was named Mary Katherine Agnes Colleen Patricia Marion Margaret Kathleen O'Shaugnessey. Back when I was a lad, working as a caddie, I carved her name in one of those trees right over there."

"Whatever happened?" asked his friend.

"The tree fell on me."

◆ ◆ ◆

Then there was the guy who lost only two golf balls all season. Ironically, he was putting at the time.

Golf is a game in which you yell 'fore',
shoot six, and write down five.

—Paul Harvey

You have to make corrections in your game a little bit at a time. It's like taking your medicine. A few aspirin will probably cure what ails you, but the whole bottle might just kill you.

—Harvey Penick

Two guys are visiting the 19th Hole after playing on a public course that was hardly reminiscent of Pebble Beach.

Complaining about it, one guy says to the other, "You know, it wasn't always like this. I once lived the life of Riley...membership in an exclusive country club, vacations in the most exotic golf resorts, the most expensive clubs money could buy. You name it, I had it."

"What happened?" asked the other guy.

"Riley reported his credit cards stolen."

Duffernitions II

Golf club: a stick with a hard head at each end

Golfer: a gardener digging up someone else's lawn

Caddie: a tee totaller

Mulligan: the chance to immediately repeat a mistake

Golf: a game where everyone in front is too slow and everyone behind is too fast

Sunday: a day on which we all bow our heads. Some of us are praying and some of us are putting and some of us are praying over a putt.

Golf: eighteen intervals of frustration mixed with several columns of poor arithmetic

Summer: that time of the year to be out on the golf course to lie in the sun

Civil War golf: out in 61 and back in 65

Every time I have the urge to play golf I lie down until the urge passes.

—Sam Levenson

Bumper Snickers

I'D RATHER BE DRIVING MY GOLF BALL

GOLFERS EXPRESS THEMSELVES TO A TEE

IF YOU DON'T LIKE THE WAY I DRIVE, YOU OUGHT
TO SEE ME PUTT

I'D RATHER BE GOLFING
*(To which an annoyed motorist might think,
"Then get the heck off the road.")*

GOLF COURSES ARE OFTEN GROUNDS
FOR DIVORCE

GOLF SEPARATES THE MEN FROM THE POISE

CAUTION: GOLFER AT WHEEL- DRIVER IN TRUNK

I BRAKE FOR ANIMALS BUT SINK BIRDIES

MY OTHER CAR IS A GOLF CART

And then there was the Romeo golf pro who usually started the ladies out on the irons and gradually worked them into the woods.

◆ ◆ ◆

Q: How is a wedding ring like a bag of golf clubs?

A: Both are instruments of eternal servitude.

◆ ◆ ◆

Mike: Do you know of any way I could take 10 or 12 strokes off my game?

Kirk: Yeah, quit on seventeen.

Golf kept me from taking an honest job.

My theory is never work for a living if you

don't have to.

—Don January

You can talk to a fade, but a hook won't listen.

—Lee Trevino

Out on the golf course, a businessman was playing golf with a priest when a sudden storm blew up.

The desperate pair found shelter in an old toolshed with a leaky roof and, as lightning struck all around them, they saw a roaring tornado bearing down on the shed.

Frantic, the businessman shrieked, "Father, can't you do something?"

"Sorry," the priest replied. "I'm in sales, not management."

◆ ◆ ◆

Then there was the bachelor who preferred golf to women. But he finally found the love of his life and got married. You might say he learned to put his heart before the course.

Freddy: I say old boy, how do you make any money lugging around people's golf bags?

Teddy: I don't. The real money comes from backing up what they claim is their score.

◆ ◆ ◆

An executive who often left to play golf during business hours told his secretary to advise all callers that he was away from his desk. A golfer who was part of the executive's foursome forgot where they were playing on this particular day so he called the secretary. Loyal to a fault, she'd only say that her boss was away from his desk.

Finally, the exasperated golfer said, "Look, just tell me. Is he five miles or ten miles away from his desk?"

Golf is the most fun you can have without taking your clothes off.

—Chi Chi Rodriguez

Most people play like Magellan. They're all over the world.

—Bob Toski

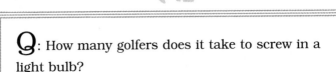

Q: How many golfers does it take to screw in a light bulb?

A: Two. One to do it and another to tell him he looked up.

◆ ◆ ◆

As he finished the fourth hole, the frustrated golfer turned to his smart aleck caddy and said, "Kid, I'm tired of your sarcasm. When we get back to the clubhouse, I'm going to report you to the pro for being such a wiseguy."

"No problem, chief," retorted the caddie, "because by the time we get back, I'll be old enough to get a real job."

Of course you've heard about the foursome that was so bad they called themselves 'The Bronchitis Brothers' because they were just a bunch of hackers.

◆ ◆ ◆

Two salesmen are out on the links talking shop.

The first salesman says, "I made some valuable contacts today."

The second salesman says, "I didn't write any orders, either."

Golf, in fact, is the only game in the world in which a precise knowledge of the rules can earn one a reputation for bad sportsmanship.

—Patrick Campbell

I owe a lot to my parents, especially my mother and father.

—Greg Norman

Just before teeing off a guy says, "I used to have an embarrassing problem with topping the ball every time I teed off. But I got help."

With that, he takes a mighty swing and the ball dribbles about three feet off the tee.

"I thought you said you got help," his golfing partner says.

"I did. I'm not embarrassed anymore."

◆ ◆ ◆

They were at the 19th Hole, watching the live telecast of the British Open when someone says, "Turn up the sound."

Someone else says, "Ssssh...not while Faldo is putting."

B ernice: How was your game, dear?

Horace: Let's put it this way. By the time I finished, all the flags on the greens were flying at half-mast.

◆ ◆ ◆

" O h honey, are you going to play golf again?"

"Come now, sweetheart. You know I play with Bob, Carl and Bill every Saturday."

"Well, occasionally you might consider skipping a Saturday to help me with the shopping, housework and the kids," said the husband.

Let's face it, 95 percent of this game is mental. A guy plays lousy golf, he doesn't need a pro, he needs a shrink.

—Tom Murphy

The Top Ten Ways To Tell You're A Golf Widow

10. When hubby refers to his "better half," he's talking about the back nine.

9. If you ever had to skip town after a golf bet went sour

8. He forgets your anniversary but annually marks the observance of the day he first played at Pebble Beach.

7. If you've ever had to put the 19th Hole on speed-dial

6. The only dimples he appreciates any more are on golf clubs

5. He tells you that you deserve a second honeymoon and then leaves on a golf vacation.

4. If fuzzy wedding picture in wallet is replaced with snapshot of Fuzzy Zoeller

3. His idea of renewing his vows is telling you exactly what he yelled after missing that two-foot putt.

2. You don't need Weather Channel. If he's home, it's raining.

And the NUMBER ONE way to tell if you're a golf widow...
When he says he's going out to "play a round,"
you almost wish he would.

A doctor, a lawyer and a hypochondriac form a threesome. Every chance the hypochondriac gets, he asks the doctor about his various ailments. Finally, when the hypochondriac goes to tee up on the 18th hole, the doctor turns to the lawyer and whispers, "I've been giving this guy professional consultation all afternoon. He'd have to pay $100 under normal circumstances. Do you think I should charge him?"

The lawyer responds, "Absolutely."

The next day, the doctor received a bill for $150 from the lawyer.

I wish my name was Tom Kite.

—Ian Baker-Finch,
on signing autographs

I believe my future is ahead of me.

—Chip Beck,
after his first PGA Tour win

Bart and Art have been a twosome on the links every day since they've been retired. One day, as they're putting on their golf shoes in the clubhouse, they get into a conversation about heaven and whether there are any golf courses there. They make a pact. The first one to die will come back and tell the other one. Bart dies first, and sure enough, comes back to visit Art.

Art says, "Well are there any golf courses in heaven?"

"I have good news and bad news," says Bart. "We have the ultimate golf course in the sky and play every day. In fact, there's a twosome tournament which starts tomorrow."

"So what's the bad news?"

"You're my partner."

Hacker: This is my first time playing golf. When do I use my putter?

Caddie: Some time before dark, I hope.

At the end of a terrible day on the links, Larry came up to the 18th tee with its imposing water hazard. Tremendously distraught, he turned to his caddie and said, "I can't take it any more. I'm going to drown myself in that lake."

His caddie said, "You'll never drown. You can't keep your head down long enough."

I hit two fairways— well, maybe four, but only two I was aiming at.

—John Daly

A guy went to a psychiatrist and announced, "There's nothing wrong with me, Doc, but my wife says if I don't come see you, she's getting a divorce."

"And exactly what does she think is the matter?" asked the shrink.

"Well," the new patient replied, "you see, I'm Jack Nicklaus and she seems to think there's something wrong with that."

A bit surprised, the psychiatrist asked, "Jack Nicklaus, as in the world-famous golfer?"

"Yep, that's me."

Knowing full well that the patient sitting before him was not Jack Nicklaus, the doctor prescribed three therapy sessions a week.

After two years of this intensive treatment, the psychiatrist announced to his patient, "Congratulations, you're cured."

"Congratulations for what?" grumbled his patient. "Before I came to you, I was Jack Nicklaus. Now I'm a nobody."

" **Y**ou think so much of your old golf game that you don't even remember when we were married."

"Of course I do, Bernice. It was the day I sank that thirty-foot putt."

◆ ◆ ◆

Did you hear about the golf widow who was sick and tired of her husband's obsession with the sport? After a long day on the links and at the 19th Hole, the hubby came home and found a note on the refrigerator. It said, "Went shopping. Your dinner is in the dog."

If I had my way, any man guilty of golf
would be ineligible for any office of trust
in the United States.

—H.L. Mencken

Nobody but you and your caddie care what you do out there, and if your caddie is betting against you, he doesn't care, either.

—Lee Trevino

HO-HO-HO!

Q: Why did the department store Santa have to give up golf during the Christmas season?

A: He had water on the knee- at least ten times a day.

Molly: I'm on a golf kick.

Polly: You? On a golf kick?

Molly: Yep. Whenever Wally mentions golf, I kick him.

Remember, golfers- Santa sees you when you're sleeping, knows when you're awake and is also well aware when you pull this kind of stuff:

The golfer's ball landed in a thicket of weeds in the middle of some woods, an unplayable lie if ever there was one. He tried to line it up but realized it was futile so he picked the ball up and moved it to a better position, shouting to his playing partners, "Found it." Suddenly, he had the feeling he was being watched. He turned around and saw an escaped convict whose picture had been plastered all over the newspaper.

The two men looked at each other for a long moment, then the golfer whispered, "Shhhh. I won't tell if you don't."

The devoted golfer is an anguished soul who has learned a lot about putting just as an avalanche victim has learned a lot about snow.

—Dan Jenkins

*The winds were blowing 50 mph and
gusting to 70. I hit a par 3 with my hat.*

—Chi Chi Rodriguez,
on a windy course in Scotland

A guy walks into the 19th Hole and orders two martinis. The bartender serves them and says, "If it's all the same to you, buddy, I could have made a double and used one glass."

The guy says, "Oh, I know, but my golfing partner died and, just before he did, I promised him I'd order him a drink after each round of golf."

The next week the guy comes back and says to the bartender, "I'll have a martini."

The bartender says, "And one for your buddy, too?"

He says, "Oh, no. This is for my buddy. I'm on the wagon."

Three little boys were arrested on the grounds of the country club. The security patrol had caught them picking cherries in the orchard off the fourth fairway.

They were taken to court where the kindly judge talked to them about the evils of stealing. He then asked them about their fathers and also about how they were going to keep from stealing ever again.

The first boy said, "My father's a doctor, and I'm always going to remember that eating stolen cherries can make me very sick."

The second boy said, "My father's a preacher. I'm going to pray to resist the temptation to steal."

The third boy said, "I sprained my ankle and tore my pants when I fell out of the cherry tree and since my father's a lawyer, I'm going to sue the country club."

If you think it's hard to meet new people,
try picking up the wrong ball.

—Jack Lemmon

Seve Ballesteros drives the ball into
territory Daniel Boone couldn't find.

—Fuzzy Zoeller

Miniature Golf

One-liners on the links

Golf is the most popular way of
beating around the bush.

A caddie is a lie-detector.

Golf is nature's way of telling you,
"This is what life looks like from behind a tree."

You can judge a man by the golf score he keeps.

Golf is a very powerful game- the only sport that
can convert a duck pond into a water hazard.

The one advantage bowling has over golf
is that you very rarely lose the ball.

Whoever said golf was fun
either has never played golf
or has never had any fun.

id you hear about the guy who opened a tavern for vulgar golfers? He called it Par for the Coarse.

◆ ◆ ◆

fter a day of golf, a couple was celebrating an anniversary dinner at the country club.

"Now tell me, dear," hubby began. "What would you like for your anniversary gift? A fur coat? A BMW?"

"Actually, honeybunch," said the wife, "I was going to ask for a divorce."

"Geez, I wasn't planning on spending that much!"

You know you're on the Senior Tour when your back goes out more than you do.

—Bob Bruce

Golf is played by 20 million mature American men whose wives think they are out there having fun.

　　　　　　　　　　—Jim Bishop

A guy runs into the pro shop and yells, "Quick. Do you know a cure for a terrible case of hiccups?"

Without saying a word, the pro gives the guy a swift kick to the stomach, forcing him to gasp for air.

"I bet you don't have the hiccups now," says the pro.

"No, but my partner on the first tee does."

Then there was the golfer who had to give up the game due to lung disease. He was breathing in too much sand.

A terrible golfer hits a ball into a gigantic bunker. He asks his caddie, "What club should I use now?"

The caddie says, "The club isn't the important thing. Just make sure to take along plenty of food and water."

◆ ◆ ◆

Jimmy: My dad has more golf trophies than your dad.

Billy: You're crazy! My dad's a pro.

Jimmy: Yeah, but my dad's a pawnbroker.

A golf course is the epitome of all that is purely transitory in the universe, a space not to dwell in, but to get over as quickly as possible.

—Jean Giraudoux

If there is any larceny in man, golf will

bring it out.

—Paul Gallico

A guy goes to the doctor for a checkup. Afterwards, the doctors says, "I've got good news and bad news."

The guy says, "Give me the bad news first, Doc."

"You've got an incurable disease and probably won't live more than a year."

"Geez, what could possibly be the good news?"

"I broke 80 yesterday."

◆ ◆ ◆

D id you hear about the doctor who told his patient to play 36 holes a day? He went out and bought a harmonica.

The newcomer to the course was studying the ball and its distance from the green. "What do you think?" he asked the caddie.

"Well, yesterday I caddied for Rodney Dangerfield. He hits 'em about like you. I advised him to use an eight-iron."

With that, the golfer took out his eight-iron, addressed the ball and played his shot- a shot that fell far short of the green.

The angry golfer said, "I thought you told Rodney Dangerfield to use an eight."

"I did. He didn't reach the green either."

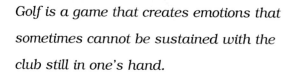

Golf is a game that creates emotions that sometimes cannot be sustained with the club still in one's hand.

—Bobby Jones

Tee Shots

*Here are some of Santa's favorite golf expressions
which are found on T-shirts as well as plaques, pillows
and other paraphernelia.*

OLD GOLFERS NEVER DIE
THEY JUST LOSE DISTANCE

GOLF IS NOT A MATTER OF LIFE AND DEATH
IT'S MUCH MORE IMPORTANT THAN THAT

HE WHO HAVE THE FASTEST CART
NEVER HAVE TO PLAY BAD LIE

GOLFERSWHOTALKFASTSWINGFAST

GOLF IS FLOG SPELLED BACKWARD

I'M NOT OVER THE HILL
I'M JUST ON THE BACK NINE

I ONLY PLAY GOLF ON DAYS THAT END IN Y

"I heard you play golf. What's your handicap?"

"A wife and three children."

◆ ◆ ◆

Harry was going by a large and deep bunker when he heard muffled cries for help. Peering down into the trap, he saw his buddy Larry trapped under an overturned golf cart.

"I think my leg is broken," groaned Larry.

"Does our lawyer know you're here?" called Harry.

"No, nobody does."

"Great," said Larry, climbing down into the trap. "Move over."

Some hotel rugs are impossible to putt.

—Tom Watson

*Why am I using a new putter? Because
the old one didn't float too well.*

—Craig Stadler

An aggressive salesman was at a restaurant with an important customer when he spotted Arnold Palmer dining across the room. Aware that his client was a golf nut, he figured he'd try to score some points. The salesman excused himself, went over to Palmer's table and said, "Pardon me, Mr. Palmer, but I've got a gigantic business deal in the works. My customer is a big fan of yours. If you'd stop by my table and just say, 'Hi, Joe,' this could put me over the top."

Palmer nodded his head and went back to his meal. When he finished, he went over to the salesman's table, tapped him on the back and said, "Hi, Joe."

Without looking up, the salesman snapped back, "Later, Arnie. Can't you see I'm eating?"

The clubhouse attendant answered the telephone, "Golf Club."

"Is my husband there?" asked a female caller.

"No, he's not."

"How can you say that when I haven't even told you his name?"

"Simple. It's a club rule. The husband's never here when his wife telephones."

"Like my game, caddie?"

"Not bad, sir. But I still prefer golf."

The toughest hole is the nineteenth. I just can't get through it. It takes the longest time to play.

—Craig Stadler

Golf appeals to the idiot in us and the child. What child does not grasp the simple pleasure-principle of miniature golf? Just how childlike golf players become is proven by their frequent inability to count past five.

—John Updike

The priest lined up his shot and announced to his caddie, "I'll take a full swing and pray that the wind dies down."

When the ball fell right into a sand trap, the priest complained, "Obviously, the Lord wasn't listening."

"Maybe," the caddie said, "but in my church, when we pray, we keep our heads down."

◆ ◆ ◆

A golf ball is a golf ball—
no matter how you putt it.

HO-HO-HO!

Duffer: What do you think I should give my caddie for Christmas?

Partner: Your clubs.

A duffer was standing in front of the church one Sunday morning, carrying his golf bag on his shoulder and trying to decide whether to worship or head out to the golf course. As he stood there, the clergyman approached him, tapped him on the back and said, "Excuse me... mind if I pray through?"

My car absolutely will not run unless my golf clubs are in the trunk.

—Bruce Berlet

How did I take a twelve? I had a long putt

for an eleven.

—Clayton Heafner

A very attractive but ill-intended young woman made it a practice to hang around the exclusive country club looking to settle down with a very rich and very old man. She found her man in J.P. Fotheringham, the 92 year-old financier. Sure enough, she and J.P. tied the knot.

Within months, J.P. became ill. As his condition worsened, the old duffer was advised to make a new will. He asked his wife, "Honey, what should I do about my estate?"

She gently hugged him and cooed, "J.P, I think you should leave all of your worldly possessions to your greatest source of comfort."

Just a few days after his rewritten will was made, the old man died. At the reading of his will, his wife learned that he left 20 million dollars to his country club.

A man of the clergy was playing golf one Sunday morning. God and Moses were watching from heaven. God said, "I'll take care of him for playing on this day of worship when he should be at church."

The man teed off on the first hole. God blew up a ferocious wind which swept the ball 400 yards right into the cup for a hole-in-one.

Moses asked, "What kind of punishment is that?"

God replied, "Ah, but who is he going to tell?"

I'm not concerned about getting in the record books. A good obituary doesn't exactly excite me.

—JoAnne Carner

A guy applies for a sales position with a big golf equipment manufacturer. While he's waiting for the interview, the receptionist tells him, "You seem like a nice guy. Let me give you a tip. My boss is very sensitive about the fact that he doesn't have any ears. At some point, he's going to ask you if you notice anything odd about him. Whatever you do, don't make any mention of the ears."

The guy thanks the receptionist for the advice and goes in for the interview. Well, the boss is very impressed with the guy's resume, his knowledge of the game in general and of golf gear in particular. But sure enough, at one point the boss says, "Tell me. Do you notice anything different about me?"

The guy looks at the boss and responds, "Well, now that you mention it, I can tell you're wearing contact lenses."

"That's amazing. I like perceptiveness in my employees. But how on earth did you know I wear contacts?"

"Easy. You'd be wearing glasses if you had any ears."

"You're a lazy, no-good-for-nothing!" snarled the rich Texan to his Ivy League son. "Do you reckon to spend all of your time traipsing around golf courses?"

"Actually, no, Dad. I was hoping you'd get me my own golf cart."

◆ ◆ ◆

Charlie and Will were watching a funeral procession.

"What a shame," said Charlie. "Old Ben was practicing with his eight-iron in his backyard when he knocked the ball through the bedroom window and killed his wife!"

"Well, what do you know?" said Will. "I have problems with my eight-iron, too."

If I had known it was going in the water,
I wouldn't have hit it there.

—Mike Reid

Belly dancers would make great golfers.

They never move their heads.

—Phil Rodgers

Taking some well deserved time off from their heavenly duties, Moses and St. Peter hit the links to indulge themselves in a game of golf. Moses teed up and hit a beautiful shot right down the fairway to the green about two feet from the hole. St. Peter, however, whacked a bad hook which disappeared into the woods. Moses was smiling smugly when an eagle emerged from high over a nearby Interstate and dropped the ball into the exhaust stack of a passing tractor-trailor. The pressure buildup soon shot the ball back into the air where it was struck by lightning from some low-lying clouds. That sent the ball careening off several chimneys and it ricocheted right back to the golf course, landed on the green and rolled right into the hole. Moses sighed, turned to a smiling St. Peter and said, "Oh, c'mon- not when we're playing for money!"

Two fellows who had seen a lot of Christmas seasons were out rocking on the porch of the rest home talking about golf.

"You know, Jake, I have a powerful hankering to play again. The trouble is my eyesight's gone and I can't hardly see across the room anymore."

"No problem, George," says Jake. "We'll go golfing together. Even though I'm 94, I still have good vision." The next morning, Jake and George arrive at the golf course and George tees up for his first drive in 20 years. He takes a tremendous swing and the ball goes flying down the fairway.

"Okay, eagle-eye," says George, "did you see where it went?"

"Sure did," replied the 94 year-old.

"Well, where did it land?" asked George.

"I forgot."

I don't make mistakes. I make disasters.

—Bob Goalby

I'm very even-tempered on the golf course.
I stay mad all the time.

—Bob Murphy

Did you hear about the Siamese twins who wrote a book about their golfing experiences? It's called Tee for Two.

◆ ◆ ◆

Then there was the dyslexic duffer who always wondered how to flog.

◆ ◆ ◆

The duffer walks into the pro shop and says, "Pete, what can I do to lower my handicap?"

Pete the pro says, "Here, take this."

"But this is just a pencil."

"Yes, but it has an eraser attached."

B ack when Tiger Woods was only a cub his father took him to the course for his first game of golf.

"Now, son, golf is a complicated game but basically all you do is hit the ball in the direction of that flag way over there."

"Okay, Dad," said little Tiger as he teed up the ball. He let go with a magnificent swing that sent the ball straight down the fairway 275 yards to land on the green just three inches from the hole.

"What do I do now, Dad?" asked the little tyke.

"You just stroll over there and knock the ball in the hole, son. After all, that is the entire point of the whole game."

"Gee, Dad," sighed Tiger. "Now you tell me."

At my age, I don't even buy green bananas.
                    —Lee Trevino,
             then 47, at the 1987 British Open

What's nice about our tour is you can't remember your bad shots.

—Bobby Brue,
on the Senior PGA Tour

George: Hey, Charlie. You look awful.

Charlie: Yeah, I know. It's my wife. It's got me so upset I can hardly play golf.

George: What's wrong with the lady?

Charlie: You're not gonna believe this, but she thinks she's a refrigerator.

George: That's not so horrible.

Charlie: Oh yeah? She sleeps with her mouth open and the light keeps me awake.

G.O.L.F.: Goofing Off and Living Fine!

Golf Is...

...great exercise, especially climbing in
and out of the cart.

...golf. You hit the ball, you go find it.
Then you hit it again.

...an expensive way of playing marbles.

...a game where the ball lies poorly,
and the players lie well.

...a bloodless sport- if you don't count ulcers.

...about the only thing that depreciates above par.

...a puzzle without an answer.

...the toughest game to play
and the easiest to cheat at.

...a long walk punctuated with disappointments.

*I don't care to join any club that's
prepared to have me as a member.*

—Groucho Marx

"Golf, golf, golf. That's all you ever think about," griped the newlywed bride at the dinner table. "You've been on the golf course every single day of our honeymoon."

"Sweetheart," cooed her husband in his most soothing tone as he reached across the table to take her hand. "Believe me, golf is the last thing on my mind at this moment. Now please stop this silliness and let's get back to our meal. Would you please pass the putter?"

◆ ◆ ◆

Show me a good loser and I'll show you a man playing golf with his boss.

"Caddie, how are you at finding balls in the rough?"

"Quite proficient, sir."

"Good... now go find one so we can get started."

Minnie: Oh, your husband looks so sharp in his golf outfit. And with that hat, he looks like "The Shark."

Millie: Maybe he looks like "The Shark" but, take my word for it, he plays like "The Guppy."

Be funny on a golf course? Do I kid my best friend's mother about her heart condition?

—Phil Silvers

I don't trust doctors. They are like golfers. Every one has a different answer to your problem.

—Seve Ballesteros

HO-HO-HO!

"Darling," said the happy hubby as he strolled into the living room. "I've just bought a Christmas present for the person I love most in the world."

"Really?" his wife answered in an icy tone. "And how do you like your new golf clubs?"

Maybe you've heard about the duffer who's so bad he has an unplayable lie when he tees up.

Bernice and Eunice pulled up to Sally and her group and asked, "Do you mind if we play through?"

"What's the big hurry?" said Sally.

Bernice responded, "The battery in our golf cart is running down."

◆ ◆ ◆

Raster blasted a mighty drive off the first tee that sailed 400 yards, bounced once on the green and landed in the cup.

"Not bad," commented Philbin. "Now I'll take my practice shot and then we can begin."

There are two things that won't last long in this world— dogs chasing cars and pros putting for pars.

—Lee Trevino

Golf, like measles, should be caught young, for if postponed to riper years, the results may be serious.

—P.G. Wodehouse

Reverend Holmes was playing golf with some members of his congregation when he hit his ball in a sand trap for the fifth time.

He began trembling as a crimson blush of total frustration rose up his neck and face like a thermometer on an August afternoon. Through clenched teeth he managed in a low growl, "Would one of you laymen please say something appropriate?"

◆ ◆ ◆

A golfer was having the worst outing of his life with slices and hooks flying far and wide. He turned and snarled at the caddie, "I thought you said you were the best caddie in Palm Beach."

"That's right, sir. I am. The trouble is that by now, we must be in Boca Raton."

At the Sleepy Hollow golf course, a foursome approached the 11th tee where the fairway runs along the edge of the course and adjoins a highway.

Forrester teed off and sliced the ball right over the fence. It hit the front tire of a bus and bounced back onto the green and into the cup for a hole-in-one.

"How on earth did you ever get it to bounce off that bus?" asked one of his astonished buddies.

"Well, first off," he replied, "you've got to know the schedule."

Golf and women are a lot alike. You know you're not going to wind up with anything but grief, but you can't resist the impulse.

—Jackie Gleason

Putting is not golf but croquet.

—A.A. Milne

McMurphy's Laws

We all know Murphy's Law but only golfers can truly appreciate "McMurphy's Laws of the Links."

1. No matter how bad your last shot was, the worst is yet to come. This law extends far beyond the 18th hole to the course of a tournament, and ultimately, an entire lifetime.

2. Your best round of golf will be immediately followed by your worst round ever. The probability of the latter increases in direct proportion with the number of people you tell about the former.

3. Brand new golf balls are irresistibly attracted to water. The more expensive the ball, the greater the attraction.

4. "Nice lag" can be translated to "lousy putt." By the same token, "tough break" translates to "I can't believe you missed that last one, bonehead."

5. Palm trees eat golf balls.

6. Sand is alive. It's an evil, malevolent presence which exists solely to make golfers' lives miserable. Sand is Demon Dust.

7. Golf balls never bounce off trees back into play. If one ever does happen to, you can bet the Devil will be teeing off in six inches of snow.

8. There is a point on every golf course that is the absolute furthest from the clubhouse. You'll know you are there when your cart runs out of juice.

9. The person you would most hate to lose to will always be the one who beats you.

10. Golf should be sworn off at least three times a month...and sworn at the rest of the time.

*My family was so poor they couldn't afford
any kids. The lady next door had me.*

—Lee Trevino

Lonnie: I'll never play golf with my banker
again.

Terry: Why not?

Lonnie: Every time I yell "Fore," he yells "Closure."

◆ ◆ ◆

Bob Hope told this story about meeting Charlie
Boswell, the blind golfer.

"I'll be happy to play a round with you," said
Hope. "If you like we can even make a small
wager."

Boswell said, "Fine, I'll bet you a $100 Nassau."

"Ok," said Hope. "What time do we tee off?"

Boswell responded, "Two o'clock in the
morning."

Strict Rules of Golf:

Never leave your opponent with the sole responsibility for thinking of all the things that could possibly go wrong with his shot.

Any four-day stretch of perfect weather will always begin on a Monday.

The score a player reports on any hole should be regarded as an opening offer.

Whenever a priest, a minister and a rabbi play golf together, it always results in an amusing story.

Golf is a game whose aim is to hit a very small ball into an even smaller hole, with weapons singularly ill-designed for the purpose.

—Winston Churchill

I'd like to see the fairways more narrow.

Then everybody would have to play from

the rough, not just me.

—Seve Ballesteros

A woman asks her husband, "If I died, would you remarry?"

He responds, "Probably."

"And would she be your golfing partner, too."

"I guess so."

"You wouldn't give her my clubs, would you?"

"Heck, no. She's a left-hander."

W hy can't we tell you the one about the golfer who lost 288 balls?

It's too gross.

Did you hear the one about the dentist who loved to play golf. Every time he approached the hole he said, "Would you open a little wider please?"

◆ ◆ ◆

Charley: So what's your handicap?

Harley: Ten.

Charley: Honestly?

Harley: What's honesty got to do with it?

◆ ◆ ◆

Then there was the skinflint who quit playing golf but took it up again eleven years later. He found his ball.

Some of us worship in churches, some in synagogues, some on golf courses.

—Adlai Stevenson

*Bad sausage and five bogeys will give
you a stomach ache every time.*

—Miller Barber

Barney's on the 18th hole with two golf balls left, an old one and a new one. His tee shot has to go over a lake and he can't make up his mind which ball to play.

All of the sudden, the clouds part and a heavenly voice bellows, "Have faith. Play the new ball."

Barney can't believe his ears, but he's not about to doubt what he just heard, so he tees up the new ball. Once again, a voice from above roars, "Take a practice swing."

Barney scratches his head, but going along with the divine advice, takes his usual hacker's swing. Just as he's about to hit the ball, the clouds part one more time and the voice says, "Play the old ball!"

Here's a favorite of every member of the North Pole Golfer's Association:

On the craggy far north coast of Scotland, McGee and McDuff were finishing up eighteen holes. A 40-knot northeast gale was blowing, whipping waves to a briny foam which was wind-driven across the course and stinging the players' eyes. The sea mist made visibility but a few yards. The temperature dropped to freezing and the course became extremely slippery. At the same time, frost was forming on the players and their equipment.

Towering waves crashed over the low bluffs and threatened to wash McGee and McDuff into the stormy sea but still they played on, occasionally stopping to snap icicles off their beards.

Finally managing to putt out against the howling wind, the golfers hefted their bags and headed for home.

"Same time next week, McGee?" asked McDuff.

"Aye," replied McGee, "weather permitting."

I don't say my golf game is bad; but if I

grew tomatoes, they'd come up sliced.

—Miller Barber

The guy was a first rate on-the-course and off-the-course louse.

When he died, he went to Hell. His eternal punishment was to serve as a caddie for the Devil. This was not your normal golf bag toting duty. The Devil plays with a hot hand...oven-heated golf clubs and balls.

Just as the guy is prepared to caddie for the first time in Hell, he sees a former playing partner, a hideously ugly man, on the first tee with a beautiful woman.

The eternally damned caddie mutters out loud, "Why do I have to suffer like this when that guy gets to spend his time with a gorgeous woman like that?"

The Devil hears him and says, "Who do you think you are to question that woman's punishment?"

The tournament wasn't going well for the pro and on the 12th green after missing a three-foot putt, he cut loose with a colorful cuss word.

When he turned around, he discovered one of the tournament marshals standing right behind him, scowling.

"Now, now...you know you're not supposed to use profanity on the course," admonished the marshal. "I'm afraid I'll have to fine you a hundred dollars."

"A hundred bucks for one little slip of the tongue? Are you serious?" protested the player.

"Yes, I'm afraid I am."

With that, the pro reached into his wallet, pulled out 500 dollars and handed it to the official.

"What's this for?" asked the puzzled marshal.

"That's a hundred to cover the fine and four hundred extra for what I'm about to say to you!"

Golf's format is fair, but the odds are terrible.

—Beau Baugh

*The way I putted, I must have been
reading the greens in Spanish and putting
them in English.*

—Homero Blancas

An expectant mother who was a couple of weeks overdue was told by her doctor to walk as much as possible every morning until the baby came. The M.D. also advised her husband that he should go along just in case anything started.

"Alright, Doc," replied the husband. "But would it be okay if she carries my clubs while she walks?"

◆ ◆ ◆

Peter the golfing punster went to a sporting goods store and bought a dozen golf balls.

The cashier asked, "Shall I wrap them for you, sir?"

Peter replied, "No thanks. I'll just drive them home."

Salesman: These new clubs will take ten strokes off your game.

Duffer: Great! I'll take two sets.

♦ ♦ ♦

Bill: I've been taking lessons, you know.

Will: Yes, and you've got a picture book swing. It's just too bad some of the pages are missing.

♦ ♦ ♦

Q: What goes 'putt, putt, putt'?

A: A lousy golfer

Golf is a game of expletives not deleted.

—Dr. Irving Gladstone

I was three over: one over a house, one over a patio, and one over a swimming pool.

—George Brett

A doctor asks his patient, "What's your problem?"

The patient replies, "I've got two problems. I'm tense and I'm nauseous."

"I've got just the remedy. If you play golf, stop. If you don't, start."

◆ ◆ ◆

"Oh, gosh. Here comes Mr. Finkle again," said Carl the caddie to his buddy, Hank. "He always gets you as his caddie, doesn't he? That's too bad. He plays so poorly."

"Aw, it's not so bad," replied Hank. "After all, I get to see parts of the course I've never seen before."

R alph played golf regularly with his minister so he was always mindful of his language.

One day though, his game was so bad that when he blew a two-foot putt on the 17th green, he let go with a string of expletives that wilted every blade of grass.

His minister, obviously disapproving of Ralph's display of temper, intoned, "I have found that the best golfers never use foul language."

To which Ralph replied, "Of course not. What the #$@%&!# do they have to cuss about?"

Golf: A game in which a ball one and a half inches in diameter is placed on a ball 8,000 miles in diameter. The object is to hit the small ball but not the larger.

—John Cunningham

You can judge a man by the golf score he keeps.

—Anonymous

Terry and Jerry were on the golf course but Jerry wasn't playing his usual game.

"What's wrong?" asked Terry.

"I guess I'm just preoccupied," replied Jerry. "I got a letter today concerning a rich uncle and a great deal of money."

"Why should that affect your game?" queried Terry.

"Because," answered Jerry, "it was Uncle Sam sending me my tax bill."

◆ ◆ ◆

"I haven't seen my husband in eight years."

"I know how you feel. My husband took up golf, too."